American
Family and Friends
2
Workbook

Naomi Simmons

OXFORD
UNIVERSITY PRESS

MW00711792

Great Clarendon Street, Oxford, OX2 6DP, United Kingdom

Oxford University Press is a department of the University of Oxford.
It furthers the University's objective of excellence in research, scholarship,
and education by publishing worldwide. Oxford is a registered trade
mark of Oxford University Press in the UK and in certain other countries

© Oxford University Press 2015

The moral rights of the author have been asserted

First published in 2015

2019 2018 2017 2016 2015

10 9 8 7 6 5 4 3 2 1

No unauthorized photocopying

All rights reserved. No part of this publication may be reproduced, stored
in a retrieval system, or transmitted, in any form or by any means, without
the prior permission in writing of Oxford University Press, or as expressly
permitted by law, by licence or under terms agreed with the appropriate
reprographics rights organization. Enquiries concerning reproduction outside
the scope of the above should be sent to the ELT Rights Department, Oxford
University Press, at the address above

You must not circulate this work in any other form and you must impose
this same condition on any acquirer

Links to third party websites are provided by Oxford in good faith and for
information only. Oxford disclaims any responsibility for the materials
contained in any third party website referenced in this work

ISBN: 978 0 19 481605 2

Printed in China

This book is printed on paper from certified and well-managed sources

ACKNOWLEDGEMENTS

Cover and title page illustration by: Tomek Giovanis and Christos Skaltsas

Illustrations by: Kathy Baxendale pp.20, 68; Andy Catling pp.44, 124; Simon
Clare pp.11, 19, 27, 31 (t), 35, 43, 51, 55 (b), 59, 67, 75, 79, 82 (b), 83, 91, 99,
103 (t), 107, 115, 123; Chris Embleton-Hall/Advocate Art pp.7, 8, 10, 16 (b), 18,
24, 32, 34, 40, 42, 48, 50, 54, 55 (t), 58, 64, 66, 72, 74, 76, 78, 79 (b), 80 (b), 88,
90, 93, 96, 102, 103 (b), 104, 106, 112, 114, 120, 122, 127, 128 (b), 129, 130, 131,
132, 133, 134, 135, 136; Amanda Enright/Advocate Art pp.28, 92, 100, 101;
Tomek Giovanis and Christos Skaltsas pp.4, 5, 17 (b), 57 (b), 71, 105, 113, 121,
128 (t); Andrew Hamilton pp.16 (t), 26, 30, 31 (b), 39, 56, 80 (t), 82 (t), 118; John
Haslam pp.14, 38, 62, 86, 110, 111; Dusan Pavlic/Beehive Illustration pp.6, 9,
12, 17 (t), 23, 25, 33, 41, 46, 49, 52, 53, 57 (t), 60, 65, 73, 81, 89, 94, 95, 97, 108,
116, 126; Lisa Smith/Sylvie Poggio Artists Agency pp.36, 84; Jo Taylor/Sylvie
Poggio Artists Agency p.98

*The publisher would like to thank the following for their permission to reproduce
photographs and other copyright material:* Alamy pp.94 (bending to touch toes/
DP RF), (breath in cold weather/DP RM), (anatomical heart/Jiri Hubatka),
119 (riding a camel/imagebroker); Bridgeman pp.47 (Van Gogh self-portrait/
Self portrait, 1889 (oil on canvas), Gogh, Vincent van (1853-90)/Musee d'Orsay,
Paris, France), (Van Gogh self-portrait with straw hat/Self Portrait with Straw
Hat, 1888 (oil on canvas), Gogh, Vincent van (1853-90)/Private Collection),
(Van Gogh self-portrait as painter/Self Portrait as a Painter, 1888 (oil on
canvas), Gogh, Vincent van (1853-90)/Van Gogh Museum, Amsterdam,
The Netherlands/De Agostini Picture Library); Corbis p.47 (Van Gogh
self portrait/Bettmann); Getty pp.46 (face close-up/Mint Images – Norah
Levine), 94 (anatomical muscles/Science Photo Library – SCIEPRO); iStock
pp.70 (rubber ducks/philipdyer); Oxford University Press pp.46 (woman's face/
Dragon Images), (hand mirror/Stockbyte); Shutterstock pp.46 (artist and easel/
Diego Cervo), (painting/Boyan Dimitrov), 70 (sinking/nikolay100), 94 (oxygen
mask/Kamira), 119 (scene from Arctic/Volodymyr Goinyk), (big rocks in the
desert/Spitzkoppe), (desert sand dune/David Steele)

DVD stills courtesy of Oxford University Press Video Department: pp.15, 39, 63, 87, 111

Contents

1 Write.

| Tim | brown | long | short | ~~Rosy~~ | green | curly | Billy |

① Her name's ___Rosy___ .

She has _____ hair.

She has _____ eyes.

② His name's _____ .

He's Rosy's cousin.

He has _____ hair.

He has _____ eyes.

③ His name's _____ .

He's Rosy's brother.

He has _____ hair.

2 Find and circle the family words.

| mom | dad | ~~brother~~ | cousin | grandma | grandpa |

brothercousingrandmamomgrandpadad

1 Write your name. Circle the correct word and write. Then draw yourself.

1 My name's _____.

2 I'm _____.

| six   seven   eight |

3 _____ hair.

| blond   brown   black   red |

4 I have _____ hair.

| long   short |

5 I have _____ hair.

| straight   curly |

6 I have _____ eyes.

| brown   blue   gray   green |

Order the words. Match.

1 Rosy's This . mom is

This is Rosy's mom. [c]

2 dad is This Rosy's .

_____ [ ]

3 . cousin Tim is Rosy's

_____ [ ]

1 Match.

1 Hello.   b   a I'm seven.

2 How are you?   ☐   b Hi.

3 What's your name?   ☐   c Bye

4 How old are you?   ☐   d I'm fine, thank you.

5 Goodbye.   ☐   e My name's Jasmin.

2 Write.

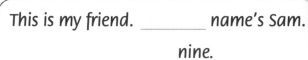

Her   His   He's   She's

This is my sister. _Her_ name's Jasmin. _____ seven.

This is my friend. _____ name's Sam. _____ nine.

3 Find and circle the days of the week. Write.

Sunday   Monday   ~~Tuesday~~   Wednesday   Thursday   Friday   Saturda

T	S	a	t	u	r	d	a	y	S
h	★	★	★	★	★	★	★	★	u
u	★	T	u	e	s	d	a	y	n
r	★	F	r	i	d	a	y	★	d
s	★	★	★	★	★	★	★	★	a
d	W	e	d	n	e	s	d	a	y
a	★	★	★	★	★	★	★	★	★
y	★	★	★	M	o	n	d	a	y

Today is _____ .

1 Count and write. | There is   There are |

1 <u>There are two</u>   cars.   2 _____ train.

3 _____ balls.   4 _____ puzzle.

5 _____ teddy bear. 6 _____ kites.

Write the missing words and numbers.

 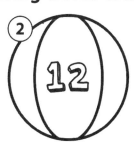 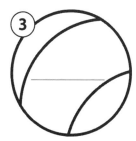   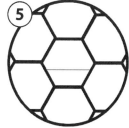

eleven   <u>twelve</u>   thirteen   _____   fifteen

 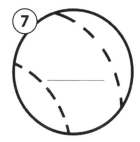  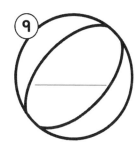 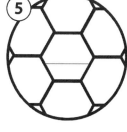 

_____   seventeen   _____   nineteen   _____

1 Find and circle the words.

| coat hooks | pencil cases | ~~classroom~~ | computers | table | board |

①  d(classroom)opl

②  acltablebi

③  jbcoathookswq

④  skocomputers

⑤ 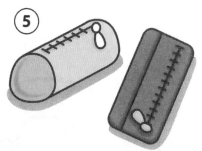 xpencilcasest

⑥ 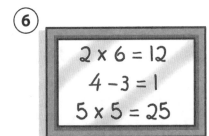 upboardzx

2 Look at the numbers in Exercise 1 and write.

1 Look at this ___classroom___ .

2 There is a new _____ .

3 There are new _____ .

4 There are new _____ .

5 There are new _____ .

6 There is a new _____ .

1 Match.

1 this [d]   2 that [ ]   3 these [ ]   4 those [ ]

2 Match.

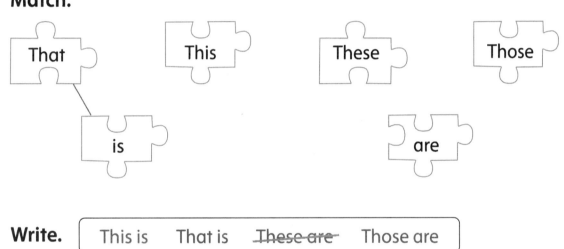

That   This   These   Those

is   are

3 Write.   This is   That is   ~~These are~~   Those are

1
These are
tables and chairs.

2
_____
coat hooks.

3
_____
a computer.

4
_____
a board.

1 Find and circle the words.

picture   poster   ~~cabinet~~   drawers

c a b i n e t p i c t u r e p o s t e r d r a w e r s

2 Look and write.

drawers   poster   ~~picture~~   chair   board
pencil case   books   computer   coat hooks

①

②

③

④

⑤

⑥

⑦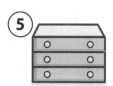

⑧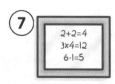

⑨

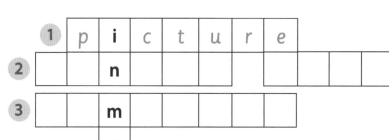

1 p i c t u r e
2   n
3   m
       y
4   c
       l
5   a
       s
6   s
7   r
8   o
9   o
       m

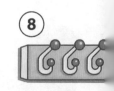

1 **Write the missing letters.**

a _b_ __ d e __ __ __ i __ k l __ __ __ __
p __ __ s t __ w __ y __

2 **Say the word. Say the sound. Circle the beginning letter.**

1. b (h) g
2. l d k
3. g y j
4. o a c
5. r p g
6. o w u
7. t b d
8. g h y
9. t s z
10. o a e

3 **Match the capital and small letters.**

g   b   e   r   h   t

B   E   G   H   R   T

Skills Time!

Reading

1 Read.

My name's Layla. I'm in class 2A. This is my classroom. The tables are long. There's a big board and there are two computers. There are big posters on the wall. There are pictures too. Can you see my picture? It's a picture of my family. My teacher is Miss Green. She's very nice.

2 Read again. Circle five things in Layla's classroom.

3 Circle the incorrect word. Then write the sentence correctly.

1 The girl's name is (Tina.)   *The girl's name is Layla.*

2 She's in class 4B.

3 The tables are short.

4 There's a small board.

5 There are four computers.

6 Layla's picture is of her friends.

7 The teacher's name is Miss White.

Writing

1 Write the sentences again with capital letters.

1 this is layla.   This is Layla.

2 layla's teacher is miss green. _____

3 his name's tim.   _____

4 rosy is tim's cousin.   _____

5 billy is her little brother. _____

6 they're a happy family.   _____

 **About me!**

2 Circle the things in your classroom.

tables   chairs   board   cabinet   drawers   computer

window   door   coat hooks   boys   girls   teachers   CD player

3 Draw and write about your classroom.

This is my classroom.

_____

This is the _____ .

This _____ .

These are the _____ .

These _____ .

_____

_____

_____

Fluency Time! ①

1 Rewrite the sentences.

1 I can't find my .

I can't find my pen.

2 I can't find my  .

_____

3 Look on the .

_____

4 Look  the cabinet.

_____

2 Look and write.

| kitchen | ~~can't~~ | Thanks | Here | there | find | Look |

I ___can't___ find my shoes.

_____ in the living room.

They aren't _____.

Look in the _____.

_____ they are.

_____, Grandpa.

Now I can't _____ my hat.

Oh Lucy!

1 Watch and number in order.

2 Watch again and order the words. What does Kate say?

1 pencil case . can't find I my

I can't find my pencil case.

2 your Look . pillow under

_____

3 . there isn't It

_____

4 is . Here it

_____

5 bed your It's under .

_____

3 Talk with a friend. What's in your bedroom?

2 They're happy now!

1 Match.

1 hot   b
2 cold
3 hungry
4 thirsty
5 happy
6 sad

2 Write.

He's _____ *happy.*   She's _____ .   _____

_____   _____   _____

1 Write. They're I'm We're She's He's

1 I'm cold.

2 _____ happy.

3 _____ thirsty.

4 _____ sad.

5 _____ hungry.

2 Write. they're they we're They're Are aren't

1 Are they hot?
No, they _____.

2 Are _____ cold?
No, they aren't cold.

3 Look, _____ hungry.
Yes. They like bananas.

4 _____ happy now and _____ happy, too.

1 **Order the words. Match.**

1 . | tired | This | is | boy

This boy is tired. → d

2 hungry | . | girls | are | These

_____ [ ]

3 angry | ? | Are | they

_____ [ ]

4 cold | aren't | boys | . | These

_____ [ ]

5 . | aren't | tired | We

_____ [ ]

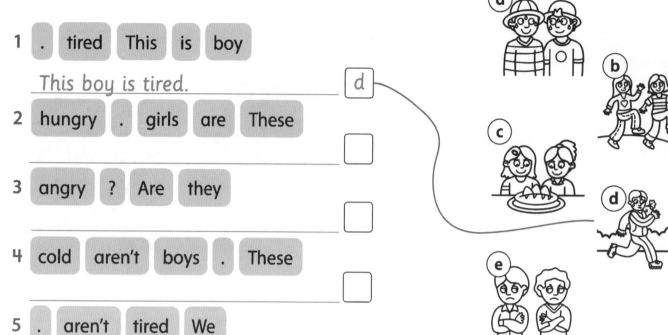

2 **Find and circle the words. Write.**

hungry

_____

_____

h	u	n	g	r	y	★	s
a	b	r	a	v	e	t	c
p	t	★	★	★	★	h	a
p	i	c	o	l	d	i	r
y	r	★	h	o	t	r	e
n	e	r	v	o	u	s	d
★	d	★	★	★	★	t	★
★	★	a	n	g	r	y	★

_____

_____

_____

_____

_____

_____

1 **Say the sound. Say the words. Circle the word that contains that sound.**

1 **sh**   chair   ~~shoes~~   thumb

2 **ch**   teacher   fish   bath

3 **th**   thumb   shoes   chair

4 **sh**   chair   bath   fish

2 **Write the missing letters.**   sh   ch   th

①
__sh__ oes

②
____umb

③
____air

④
tea____er

⑤
ba____

⑥
fi____

Write.   bath   ~~teacher~~   shoes   teacher   fish   chair

Look at my ¹_____teacher_____.

Sitting on a ²_____.

Her ³_____ are blue.

She has long, black hair.

A picture of a ⁴_____.

And a picture of a ⁵_____.

Look at my ⁶_____.

Her name's Miss Wish.

Digraphs ch sh th **Unit 2**   **19**

Skills Time!

Reading

1 Read.

My feelings

I cry when I fall over.
I cry when I am sad.
I cry when Mom is angry,
When I do something bad.

I smile when I am happy.
I smile when I am good.
I smile when I am brave,
When I do something good.

2 Write the words in the correct boxes.

happy	~~sad~~	angry	brave	bad	good

sad

3 Read again and write *T* (true) or *F* (false).

1 I cry when I am happy.   F

2 I smile when I do something good.   _____

3 I cry when I am sad.   _____

4 I smile when Mom is angry.   _____

5 I smile when I am brave.   _____

6 I cry when I do something good.   _____

Writing

1 **Write the long and short forms.**

long form	short form
1 I am happy.	*I'm happy.*
2 She is tired.	_____
3 _____	They're sad.
4 We are scared.	_____
5 _____	You're hungry.
6 I am thirsty.	_____
7 _____	He's cold.
8 They are nervous.	_____

About me!

2 **How are you feeling today? Write ✔ or ✗.**

hot ☐   cold ☐   tired ☐   hungry ☐   thirsty ☐   happy ☐

sad ☐   brave ☐   angry ☐   scared ☐   nervous ☐

3 **Draw and write about your feelings.**

	Today I'm happy.
	Today I'm _____.
	I'm _____.
	_____
	Today I'm not _____.
	I'm not _____.
	_____

Math Time!

1 Write.

whole	half	~~third~~	quarter

1 It is in three equal shapes. Each shape is a _____third_____.

2 It is in two equal shapes. Each shape is a _____.

3 There is one shape. The shape is a _____.

4 It is in four equal shapes. Each shape is a _____.

2 Read. Color the shapes.

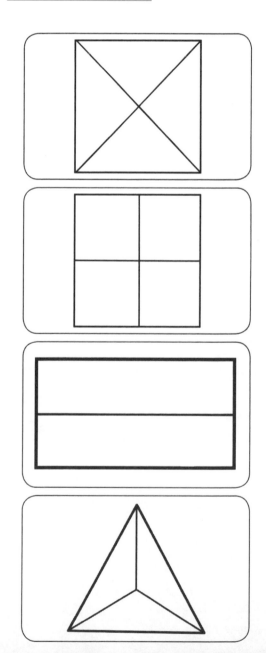

1 This square is cut into four quarters. Each quarter is a triangle. Color one quarter red.

2 This square is also cut into four quarters. Each quarter is a square. Color three quarters blue.

3 This rectangle is divided into two halves. Each half is a long rectangle. Color one half yellow and one half green.

4 This triangle is divided into three thirds. Each third is a small triangle. Color two thirds orange.

1 Listen again and write. 🔘 30

circle	diamond	third	quarter
rectangle	three quarters	half	~~square~~

1

What part of this
_____square_____ is blue?

The answer is one
_____.

2

How much of this
_____ is red?

The answer is one
_____.

3

And the _____?
What part is green?

_____
are green.

4

And this _____?
How much is orange?

The orange shape is
one _____.

2 Look at Exercise 1. Point and say.

3 I can ride a bike!

1 **What's next?**
Look, draw, and write.

| ride a bike | ~~ride a horse~~ | skate | skateboard |
| play tennis | play soccer |

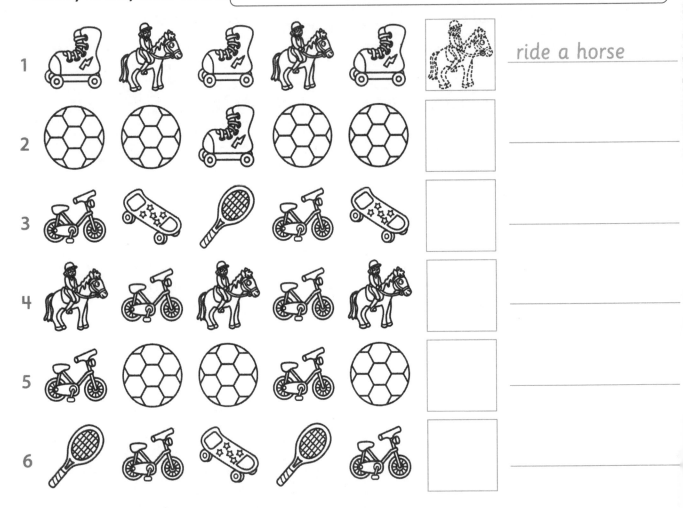

1   ride a horse

2

3

4

5

6

2 **Write the words in the correct box.**

| play tennis | skateboard | ~~ride a bike~~ | skate | play soccer |

①   ride a bike

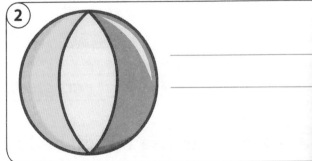

②

1 Look and write.

| No, she can't. | No, he can't. | Yes, they can. | ~~Yes, he can.~~ |
| | No, they can't. | Yes, she can. | |

①

Can he ride a bike?

Yes, he can.

②

Can she skate?

③

Can they play tennis?

④

Can they skateboard?

⑤

Can she swim?

⑥

Can he ride a horse?

2 Look again and write.

1 _He can ride a bike._

2 _____

3 _____

4 _____

5 _____

6 _____

1 Match.

1 behind   a

2 in front of   ☐

3 next to   ☐

4 between   ☐

5 on   ☐

6 under   ☐

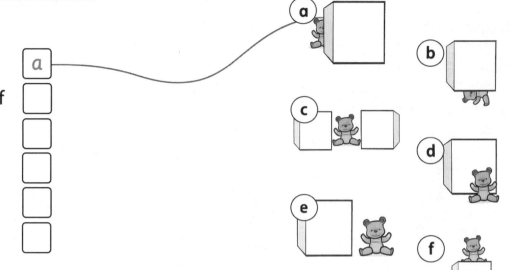

2 Write. Then number the picture.

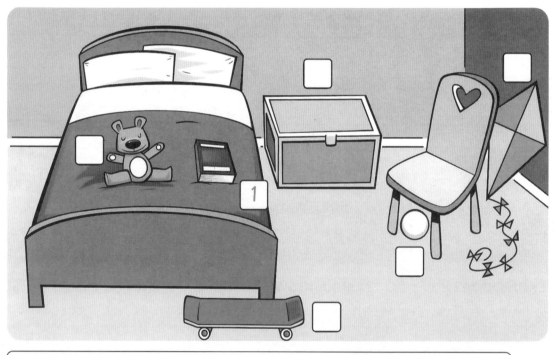

| under | ~~next to~~ | on | in front of | behind | between |

1 The book is _____ next to _____ the teddy bear.

2 The teddy bear is _____ the bed.

3 The ball is _____ the chair.

4 The kite is _____ the chair.

5 The skateboard is _____ the bed.

6 The toybox is _____ the bed and the chair.

1 **Say the sound. Say the words. Circle the word that contains that sound.**

1 **a** pen (cat) bug

2 **e** bed mop bus

3 **i** dog van fig

4 **o** pen dog pig

5 **u** bus bed cat

2 **Write the missing letters.** a e i o u

b _u_ g   c __ t   d __ g   f __ g

v __ n   p __ g   b __ s   p __ n

3 **Say the word. Look and write a word that rhymes.**

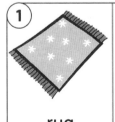 

rug   _bug_

man   _____

 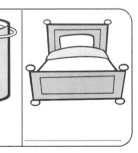

red   _____

big   _____

log   _____

Skills Time!

Reading

1 Read.

A Look at this bike. Two people can ride it. It has two wheels and it has two seats. Your mom or dad can sit in front. You can sit behind. There are four pedals. It's fun to ride this bike with your mom or dad.

B Can you ride a bike with only one wheel? This man can. The wheel is very big and it has one seat at the top. It's difficult to ride, but fun.

2 Read again. Write.

1   How many wheels does bike A have?

It has _____ .

2   How many seats does bike B have?

_____

3 Circle the incorrect word. Then write the sentence correctly.

1 Bike A: It has (one) wheels.   _It has two wheels._

2 Bike B: It has a little wheel.   _____

3 Bike A: Four people can ride this bike.   _____

4 Bike B: It has two seat.   _____

5 Bike A: You can sit between.   _____

6 Bike B: The man can't ride this bike.   _____

Writing

1 Complete using *a* or *an*.

1 This is ___an___ orange.

2 I have _____ bike.

3 He has _____ skateboard.

4 This is _____ umbrella.

5 It's _____ apple.

6 She has _____ egg.

7 I have _____ teddy bear.

8 My sister has _____ ice pop.

About me!

2 Check (✔) what you can do.

ride a bike	☐	ride a horse	☐	skate	☐	run	☐	cook	☐
play tennis	☐	play soccer	☐	swim	☐	fly	☐	dance	☐
climb	☐	skateboard	☐	sing	☐	draw	☐		

3 Draw and write about what you can and can't do.

I can play soccer.

I can _____.

I can _____.

_____

_____

I can't _____.

I can't _____.

_____

1 Write.

| That is | ~~This is~~ | these are | Those are | This is |

1

This is my bedroom.
_____ ___ my bed.

2

_____ ___ my cabinet.

3

_____ ___ my pictures.

4

And _____ ___ my toys.

Great! Let's play.

2 Read the words. Write them in the correct boxes.

hungry   ~~computer~~   scared   bike   skateboard   tired   board
skates   coat hooks   nervous   teddy bear   posters

school	feelings	toys
computer	_____	_____
_____	_____	_____
_____	_____	_____
_____	_____	_____

3 Say the words. Circle the word that contains a different sound.
Write the sound that is different.

sh	ch	th

1 _sh_

2 _____

3 _____

4 _____

4 Write.

| Yes, she is. | Yes, they are. | ~~No, he isn't.~~ | No, they aren't. |
| No, she isn't. | Yes, he is. |

Is he happy?

No, he isn't.

Is she hungry?

_____

Is he brave?

_____

Is she cold?

_____

Are they tired?

_____

Are they hot?

_____

Do you have a milkshake?

1 Number the picture.

1. ~~milkshake~~
2. salad
3. chicken
4. pizza
5. fries
6. cheese sandwich

2 Look and write.

pizza   fries   ~~salad~~   sandwich   milkshake   chicken

1.

1	s	a	l	a	d

2.

		u		

| 2 | | | n | | | | | |

3.

| 3 | c | | | | | | |

| 4 | | | | | | h | |

		t	

| 5 | | i | | | |

5.

		m	

| 6 | | | | e | |

1 Write.

| Yes, he does. | No, he doesn't. | Yes, she does. | No, she doesn't. |

1 Does the boy have a milkshake? _Yes, he does._

2 Does the girl have a milkshake? _____

3 Does he have a pizza? _____

4 Does she have fries? _____

2 Order the words. Match.

1 Do you a have pizza ?

_____ d

2 sandwiches like the They .

_____ ☐

3 doesn't He his . have fries

_____ ☐

4 hungry not . I'm

_____ ☐

1 **Write the numbers.**

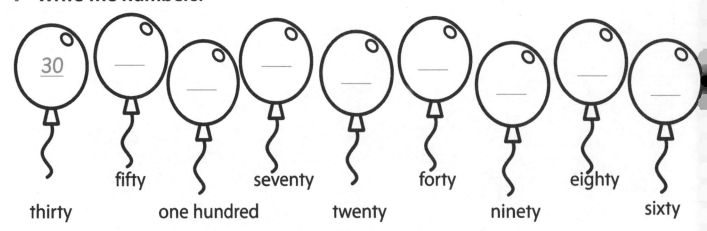

30

fifty   seventy   forty   eighty

thirty   one hundred   twenty   ninety   sixty

2 **Now write the number words in order.**

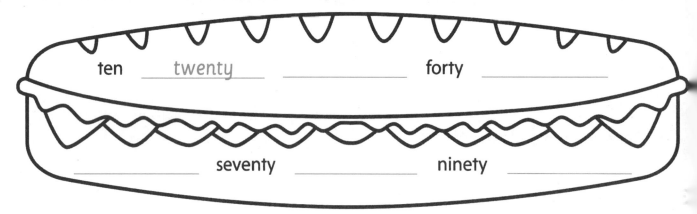

ten   _twenty_   _____   forty   _____

_____   seventy   _____   ninety   _____

3 **Look and write the numbers.**

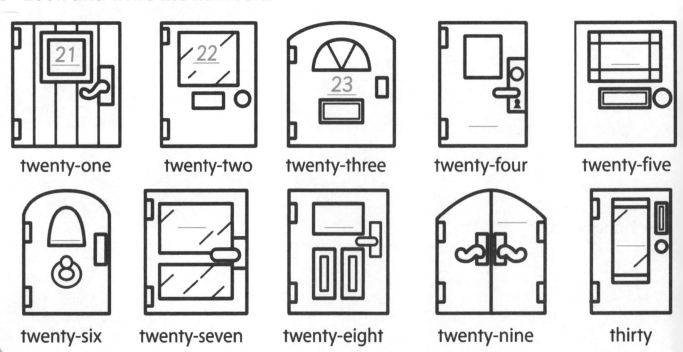

twenty-one   twenty-two   twenty-three   twenty-four   twenty-five

twenty-six   twenty-seven   twenty-eight   twenty-nine   thirty

Lesson Four Phonics

1 Say the sound. Say the words. Circle the word that contains that sound.

1 **gr**   frisbee   (grapes)   bread

2 **br**   brush   frog   grass

3 **fr**   frog   brush   bread

4 **gr**   brush   frisbee   grass

2 Circle the letters at the beginning of each word.

1    (gr)   fr   br

2   fr   br   gr

3    gr   fr   br

4 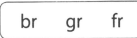   br   gr   fr

3 Write.

| juice   ~~grapes~~   frisbee   friends   grass   bread |

There are ¹ <u>grapes</u> and ² _____ ,

And ³ _____ in a glass.

Friends together,

In the green, green ⁴ _____ .

Play with a ⁵ _____ ,

Play with a ball.

The ⁶ _____ have fun

With the big, brown ball.

Consonant blends *gr br fr*   **Unit 4**   **35**

Skills Time!

Reading

1 Read.

Kate: Let's look in our lunchboxes.
Simon: That's a good idea.

Kate: Do you have a sandwich?
Simon: Yes, I do. I have an egg sandwich.

Kate: Do you have chicken?
Simon: No, I don't. But I have salad. And I have a cookie. And you?

Kate: I have a cheese and tomato sandwich. But I don't have a salad. I don't have a cookie. But I have a yogurt.

2 Read again. Check (✔) what they have.

	Simon	Kate
1 cookie	✔	
2 egg sandwich		
3 salad		
4 chicken		
5 cheese and tomato sandwich		
6 yogurt		

3 Read again and write *T* (true) or *F* (false).

1 Kate has a cookie.　　　　_F_　　2 Kate doesn't have a cookie.

3 Simon doesn't have salad.　　　　4 Kate has a salad.

5 Simon has an egg sandwich.　　　　6 Kate has a yogurt.

Writing

1 **Write . or ? at the end of each sentence.**

1 Can you skateboard   Can you skateboard?

2 I have an apple

3 Do you have a sandwich

4 No, I don't

5 Do you like yogurt

6 Does he have a pizza

About me!

2 **Circle the food you have in your lunchbox.**

salad   fries   pizza   milkshake   cheese   sandwich

yogurt   cookie   orange   apple   pear   banana   chicken

Draw and write about what's in your lunchbox.

I have a pizza in my lunchbox.

I have a   .

I have   .

I don't have   .

I   .

Fluency Time! ②

1 Look and write.

in   ~~What's~~   slowly   spell   board

1 ____What's____ this _____ English?

I don't remember.

2 It's a _____.

Speak more _____, please.

3 It's a board.

Can you _____ it, please?

b-o-a-r-d.

2 Order the words.

1 English   this   What's   in   ?

What's this in English?

2 remember   I   .   don't

_____

3 slowly   ,   more   please   .   Speak

_____

4 please   Can   ?   it   you   ,   spell

_____

1 **Watch and check (✔) the objects you see.** **DVD Practice**

a  ✔

b  ☐

c  ☐

d  ☐

e  ☐

f 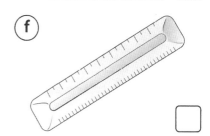 ☐

2 **Watch again. Complete and match.**

It's   spell   ~~this~~   slowly

a

1 What's _____this_____ in English?

b

2 _____ a computer.

c

3 Sorry? Speak more _____, please.

d

4 Can you _____ it?

3 **Do you remember these toys? Ask a friend.**

   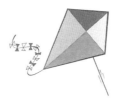

What's this in English?
I don't remember.

5 We have English!

1 Circle the words.   math   P.E.   science   music   English   ~~art~~

2 Now write.

(1)

art

(2)

(3)

(4)

(5) $2+2=4$ $3 \times 2=6$
      $6-3=3$ $4+5=9$
      $7 \times 1=7$ $5+3=8$

(6)

3 Look at the numbers on the pictures above and write.

What do you have on Monday?

I have ²_____ and ⁶_____ .

What do you have on Wednesday?

I have ³_____ , ⁴_____ , and _____ .

1 **Match. Then write.**

① These are _our_ P.E. bags.

our

② Those are _____ P.E. bags.

their

③ Those are _____ lunchboxes.

④ These are _____ lunchboxes.

2 **Match.**

	Monday	Tuesday	Wednesday	Thursday	Friday
9.00	art	English	math	science	

1 When do we have English? [b]   **a** We have art.

2 What do we have on Thursday? [ ]   **b** On Tuesday.

3 What do we have on Monday? [ ]   **c** On Wednesday.

4 When do we have math? [ ]   **d** We have science.

Write.

1 Tuesday   We have ____English____ on ____Tuesday____ .

2 Monday   We have _____ on _____ .

3 Thursday   _____

4 Wednesday _____

1 Look and write.

computer room   ~~art room~~   field   school yard   gym

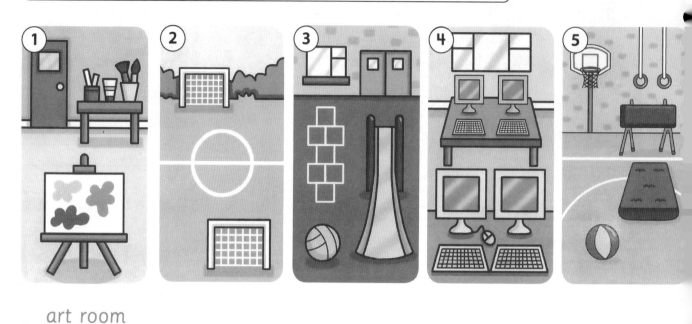

1 art room   2 _____   3 _____   4 _____   5 _____

2 Match.

1 school yard [b]   2 computer room [ ]   3 gym [ ]

4 art room [ ]   5 classroom [ ]

      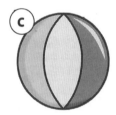      

pictures   garbage can   ball   computers   books

3 Now write.

1 We have a _____garbage can_____ in the _____school yard_____ .

2 We have _____ in the _____ .

3 _____

4 _____

5 _____

1 Say the sound. Say the words. Match.

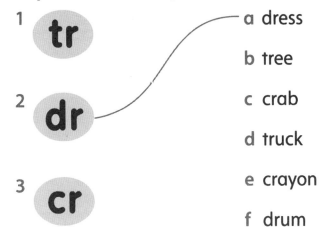

1 tr
2 dr
3 cr

a dress
b tree
c crab
d truck
e crayon
f drum

2 Write the missing letters. | dr   tr   cr |

| 1 | 2 | 3 | 4 | 5 | 6 |

_tr_ ee   ____ab   ____um   ____ess   ____ayon   ____uck

3 Write.

| drum   ~~train~~   crayons   crab   truck   dress   tree   crayons |

A ¹___train___ and a ²_____.
A ³_____ and a ⁴_____.
I draw with my ⁵_____,
And I have fun.
A girl in a ⁶_____.
A bird in a ⁷_____.
Get your ⁸_____,
And draw with me.

Reading

1 Read.

At our school we have two big school yards. This is my school yard. It is for the 1st, 2nd, and 3rd grade students. The 4th, 5th, and 6th grade students play on a different school yard.

On our school yard there is a jungle gym and a garbage can. There are squares on the school yard where we can play jumping games. The students can play ball and run around. We can also talk to our friends. We love our school yard.

2 Read again. Circle three things that are on the school yard.

3 Read again. Then write.

garbage can   ~~school yards~~   friends   squares   big   ball

1 At this school, there are two ___school yards___ .

2 The school yards are _____ .

3 In this school yard, there is a jungle gym and a _____ .

4 There are _____ for jumping games.

5 The students can play _____ .

6 The children can talk to their _____ .

Writing

1 Write the sentences with capital letters.

1 we have science on tuesday.   _We have science on Tuesday._

2 what do we have on thursday?   _____

3 do we have math on monday?   _____

4 we don't have school on saturday.   _____

5 what do we have on wednesday?   _____

6 we have art on wednesday.   _____

About me!

2 Check (✔) the school subjects you have today.

art ☐   math ☐   English ☐   science ☐   P.E. ☐   music ☐

3 Draw and write about today's subjects.

We have English.

We have _____.

We have _____.

_____

We don't have _____.

We _____.

_____

Art Time!

1 Find and circle the words.

artist   ~~mirror~~   skin   face   background

1 m e m i r r o r e l

2 o d k s k i n o e

3 o u t l f a c e e i n

4 a e i a r t i s t l m

5 l b I b a c k g r o u n d a n d

2 Write, using the words from Exercise 1.

1 Look in a mirror. You can see your

_____ .

2 It is red behind my self-portrait.
Red is the _____ .

3 I can see my face. My _____

is light brown.

4 I can see my face in a _____ .

5 Rembrandt is an _____ .

1 Listen again. Write. 🎧 65

background	pencil	dark	~~hat~~	paint
hat	light	color	paintbrushes	painting

1 Van Gogh has a yellow _____hat_____ .
   The _____ of the painting is dark blue.
   He has a _____ blue coat, too.

2 In this _____ , Van Gogh doesn't have
   a hat on. We can see _____ and
   _____ in the painting.

3 He isn't wearing a _____ .
   The background is _____ blue.

4 This is a _____ drawing. There is no
   paint and there is no _____ .

2 Look at Exercise 1. Point and say.

6 Let's play after school!

1 Match.

1 help my [b]   a swimming

2 do my ☐   b mom

3 visit my ☐   c TV

4 go ☐   d homework

5 have a ☐   e music lesson

6 watch ☐   f grandma

2 Look and write.

go swimming

Order the words. Match.

1   mom . help my I

_I help my mom._____   c

2   visit grandma I . my

_____   ☐

3   homework I my do .

_____   ☐

4   TV . don't watch I

_____   ☐

Write.

Monday

_I do my homework._____

I don't _____ .

Tuesday

I _____ .

I don't _____ .

Wednesday

_____

_____

Thursday

_____

_____

1 Circle the correct word. Write.

After school, I __listen to__ music.

write	~~listen to~~

I _____ a book.

read	listen to

I _____ with my friends.

write	play

I _____ an email.

play	write

2 Write. Then number the picture.

help	read	~~listen~~	play	write	watch

1 I ____listen____ to music.

2 I _____ a book.

3 I _____ TV.

4 I _____ an email.

5 I _____ with my friend.

6 I _____ my mom.

1 Join the sounds. Circle the sounds in the words.

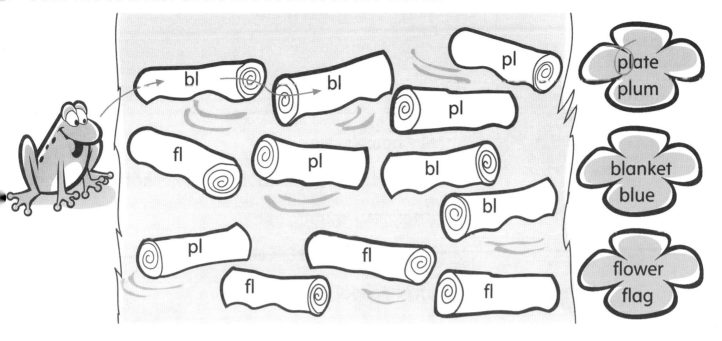

2 Say the words. Circle the sound.

  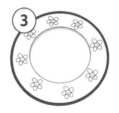  

1	2	3	4	5
fl pl (bl)	fl pl bl	fl pl bl	fl pl bl	fl pl bl

3 Write.
Plums	flower	blanket	~~Plums~~	plate

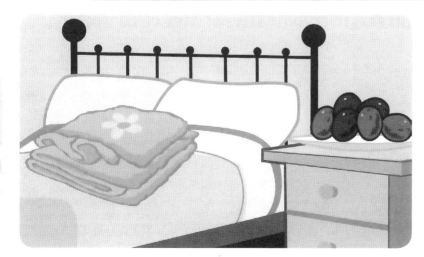

¹ _Plums_ on a plate.

² _____ on a plate.

Blue plums, black plums,

Plums on a ³_____.

A ⁴_____ on a bed.

A blanket on a bed.

There's a pretty ⁵_____

On the blanket on the bed.

Skills Time!

Reading

1 Read.

My name's Alex.

Every day after school, I do my homework and I help my mom.

I really like sport. Every Tuesday, I play soccer after school. All my friends play, too.
I love it!

Every Thursday, I visit my cousins. We play with our toys together. I have two cousins. One is a boy and his name is Zac. He's ten. The other is a girl and she's six. Her name is Abby.

2 Circle the words that are incorrect. Then write the sentences correctly.

1 I'm Tony.   I'm Alex.

2 After school, I help my sister.   _____

3 Every Tuesday, I play basketball.   _____

4 Every Wednesday, I visit my cousins.   _____

5 Zac and Abby are my friends.   _____

6 I have four cousins.   _____

7 Zac is six.   _____

8 Abby is a boy.   _____

Writing

1 Circle the verbs. Then match.

1 I (visit) my cousins. [a]

2 I play soccer. [ ]

3 I help my mom. [ ]

4 I have a music lesson. [ ]

5 We play with our toys. [ ]

6 We watch TV. [ ]

 **About me!**

Circle the things you do after school.

help my mom   do my homework   watch TV   read a book

write an email   play with my friends.   listen to music

Draw and write what you do and don't do after school.

After school, I visit my grandma.

After school, I _____

_____

I _____ .

_____

I don't _____ .

I don't _____ .

_____

1 **Write. Then color the clothes.**

| your | ~~our~~ | my | their |

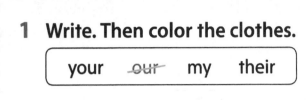

1 Let's play soccer.

These are _our_ soccer shirts. They're green.

2 These are _____ soccer shirts. They're red.

3 These are _____ soccer shorts. They're black.

4 These are _____ soccer shorts. They're yellow.

2 **Read the words. Write them in the correct boxes.**

| math | ~~twenty~~ | chicken | English | science | salad |
| forty | fries | thirty | eighty | music | pizza |

numbers	food	subjects
twenty		

3 Read and write the numbers.

24

1 The car is number twenty-four.

2 The skateboard is number eighty-one.

3 The train is number seventy-nine.

4 The doll is number thirty-seven.

5 The kite is number forty-six.

4 Complete the questions.   What   When

1 ___What___ do we have on Tuesday? We have science.

2 _____ do we have art? On Wednesday.

3 _____ do we have English? On Monday.

4 _____ do we have on Monday? We have P.E.

5 _____ do we have on Thursday? We have math.

6 _____ do we have science? On Tuesday.

5 Circle the beginning sound.

1 fr fl   2 dr gr   3 fr fl   4 br dr   5 tr dr   6 cr tr

7 Let's buy presents!

1 Find and circle the words.

present ~~cake~~ chocolate card balloon candy

cakeballoonpresentchocolatecandycard

2 Match. Then write.

chocolate ~~candy~~ balloon present cake card

① b

② ☐

③ ☐

④ ☐

⑤ ☐

⑥ ☐

ⓐ _____

ⓑ candy

ⓒ _____

ⓓ _____

ⓔ _____

ⓕ _____

1 Write.

| like | likes | don't like | doesn't like |

① I _____like_____ chocolate.

② I _____ candy.

③ She _____ balloons.

④ She _____ chocolate.

2 Read. Then write.

| likes | doesn't like | like | likes |

① Billy _____likes_____ trains and cars.

② And he _____ chocolate.

③ I _____ these balloons.

④ Billy _____ balloons.

Lesson Three Words

1 Find and circle the words.

neighbor   tie   buy   ~~pastries~~

① axpastriestp

② ieybuysas

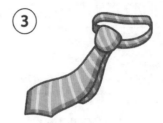
③ mptieb

④ eneighborop

2 Look and write.

cake   candy   balloon   pastries   nuts
chocolate   neighbor   tie   ~~card~~

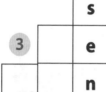
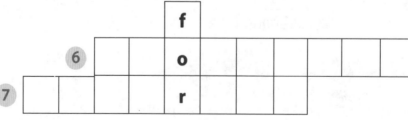
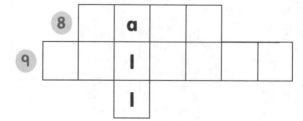

p
1 c a r d
2 e
s
3 e
4 n
t
5 s

f
6 o
7 r

8 a
9 l
l

58   Unit 7   Special days

1 Say the words. Circle the word that begins with a different sound.

1 gloves   glue   (clock)   2 slide   cloud   slippers

3 glue   clock   cloud   4 slide   gloves   glue

5 slippers   glue   slide

2 Write the missing letters.   cl   gl   sl

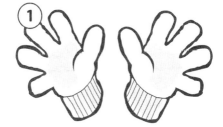      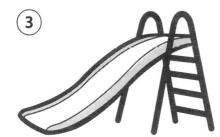

① __gl__ oves   ② ___ ock   ③ ___ ide

      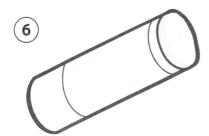

④ ___ oud   ⑤ ___ ippers   ⑥ ___ ue

3 Write.   gloves   slide   ~~slippers~~   clock   clouds

I take off my [1] __slippers__ ,

I go outside.

I put on my [2] _____ ,

And I play on the [3] _____ .

I look at the [4] _____ .

I see [5] _____ in the sky,

Time to take off my gloves,

Time to say, "Goodbye."

Skills Time!

Reading

1 Read.

How to wrap a present

This is a present for my friend Holly. It's a box of chocolates.

1 Get paper. Holly's favorite color is red, so this is red paper.
2 Put the present on the paper.
3 Fold up the paper.
4 Tape the paper.
5 Make triangles with the paper. Tape the triangles.
6 Tape pictures on the present. Holly likes flowers.
7 Write a card. My card says, "To Holly. You are a good friend. From Teresa."

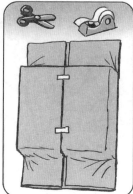

2 Read again. Put the pictures in the correct order.

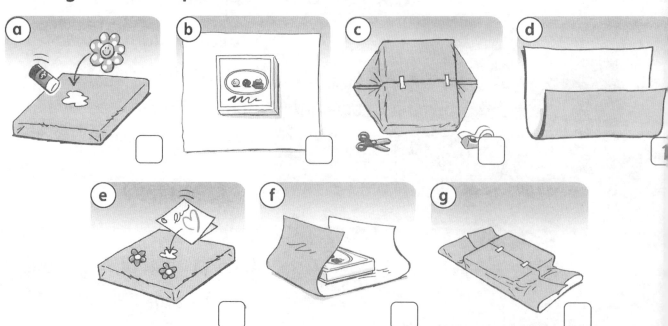

a

b

c

d

e

f

g

Writing

1 Write the long and short forms.

long form	short form
1 I do not like candy.	*I don't like candy.*
2 _____	He doesn't like balloons.
3 She does not like eggs.	_____
4 _____	I don't like tigers.
5 I do not like snakes.	_____
6 _____	My mom doesn't like cats.
7 My grandpa does not like cake.	_____

About me!

2 Think about a present for your mom. Check (✔) the things she likes.

cake ☐   books ☐   pastries ☐   nuts ☐   grapes ☐

toy cars ☐   yo-yos ☐   balloons ☐   slippers ☐   gloves ☐

3 Draw and write about presents for your mom.

[drawing box   ]

My mom likes candy.

My mom likes _____.

She likes _____.

_____

_____

She doesn't like _____.

She _____.

Fluency Time! ③

1 Write the sentences.

| bananas | apples | ~~carrots~~ | fig |

I want three carrots, please.

I want _____ .

I _____ .

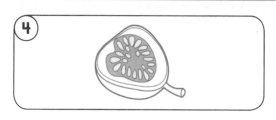

_____ .

2 Look and write.

| Anything | much | ~~Can~~ | I | want | else |

① _____Can_____ I help you?

Yes, I _____ three tomatoes, please.

② Here you are.
Anything _____ ?

Yes. _____ want two apples, please.

③ _____ else?

No, thanks.

④ How _____ is it?

Five dollars, please.

1 Watch and circle. Then number in order.

a

1 – 2 – 3   3 – 4 – 5

b

Bye!   Here you are.

c

1

two apples   (four apples)

2 Complete the sentences.

Anything   dollars   ~~want~~   Here   welcome

I _____want_____ four apples, please.

OK, 1-2-3-4. _____ else?

No, thanks. How much is it?

Two _____, please.

_____ you are.

Thank you.

You're _____. Bye!

3 Talk with a friend. What fruit and vegetables do you like? What food can you see in your market?

I like apples and carrots.

8 What time is it?

1 Write.

> get up   have breakfast   go to school   go home
> have dinner   go to bed

have dinner

2 Order the words. Look at the pictures above and match.

1 school go I to .

I go to school. [3]

2 home . go I

3 . up get I

4 dinner I . have

5 bed . I to go

6 I breakfast have .

1 Look and write.

It's seven o'clock. _____ _____

_____ _____ _____

2 Read and match.

1 He has breakfast. [c]

2 He gets up. [ ]

3 He has dinner. [ ]

4 He goes to school. [ ]

Now write the sentences in the correct order.

1 _He gets up at six o'clock._   2 He _____.

3 _____   4 _____

1 Look at the pictures and match.

1 in the morning   b   2 in the afternoon ☐

3 in the evening ☐   4 at night ☐

 a    b    c   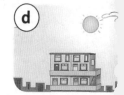 d

2 Write.

1 I have breakfast
in the morning.

2 I go to bed _____
_____.

3 I have dinner _____
_____

4 I have lunch _____
_____.

5 I get up _____
_____.

6 I play with my toys
_____

3 Now point and say.

> I have breakfast in the morning.
> I go to bed ...

1 **Say the words. Circle the word that begins with a different sound.**

1 small   smile   (sky)

2 stairs   snow   star

3 star   snow   snake

4 skates   small   sky

5 skates   small   smile

2 **Write the missing letters.** | sm   sn   st   sk |

 ①   _st_ airs

 ②   ___ile

 ③   ___ake

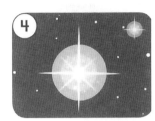 ④   ___ar

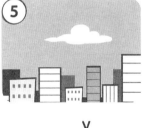 ⑤   ___y

 ⑥   ___ow

 ⑦   ___ates

 ⑧   ___all

3 **Write.** | sky   ~~snake~~   stars   snow   smile |

Look at the ¹ ___snake___

In the ² _____ .

A snake with a ³ _____ .

Watch it go.

Look at the ⁴ _____

In the night ⁵ _____ .

It's time for bed, snake.

Say, "Goodbye."

Skills Time!

Reading

1 Read.

My name's Harry and this is my dad.
In the morning, I get up at seven o'clock. My dad gets up at six o'clock.
I go to school at eight o'clock. My dad goes to work at seven o'clock.
I go to school by bus. He goes to work by car.
I go home at four o'clock in the afternoon. My dad goes home at seven o'clock in the evening.
I go to bed at eight o'clock. My dad goes to bed at eleven o'clock.

2 Read again. Write *H* (Harry) or *D* (Dad).

1 get up		D		
2 go to school go to work				
3 go by …				
4 go home				
5 go to bed				

Writing

1 Write.

| What | Where's | When | Where | ~~What's~~ | When |

1 ___What's___ your name? My name is Harry.

2 _____ his teddy bear? His teddy bear is in his bedroom.

3 _____ do you go? I go to school.

4 _____ do you have P.E.? On Tuesday.

5 _____ does she like? She likes chocolate and candy.

6 _____ does she get up? She gets up in the morning.

About me!

2 Write the times you do these things.

get up   have breakfast   go to school

have lunch   have dinner   go to bed

3 Draw and write about your day.

I get up at six o'clock.

I get up at _____.

I _____.

_____

_____

_____

Science Time!

Topic: Materials

1 Look and write.

| ~~float~~ sink air light heavy |

1 These toy ducks ____float____ on the water.

2 There is _____ inside the toy ducks.

3 Air is _____ , so the ducks float.

4 Stones are _____

5 They _____ to the bottom of the water.

2 Circle T (true) or F (false).

1 Air is heavier than water.	T	F
2 Toy ducks float on the water.	T	F
3 Stones are heavier than water.	T	F
4 Stones float on the water.	T	F
5 There is water in the toy duck.	T	F
6 Some things float and some things sink.	T	F

1 Listen again. Write. 🎧 100

> no   water   floats   ~~air~~   sink
> ~~balloon~~   float   teacher   think   you

a

I think that it floats. The balloon has _____ in it. Air is lighter than _____.

b

Yes, it _____.
You are correct.

Thank _____.

c

A balloon with _____ air.
Does it float or _____?

I _____ it sinks now.

d

Look, the _____ with no air floats, too.

Why does it _____?

Let's ask our _____.

2 Look at Exercise 1. Point and say.

Where does she work?

1 Find and circle the words.

| hospital | airport | fire station | police station | store | ~~school~~ |

1 t o l (s c h o o l) m b h

2 b p o l i c e z
   h s t a t i o n x

3 a r h o s p i t a l o u

4 c h t s t o r e t u b x

5 m k l a i r p o r t q r y

6 v f i r e p y s t a t i o n t

2 Look and write.

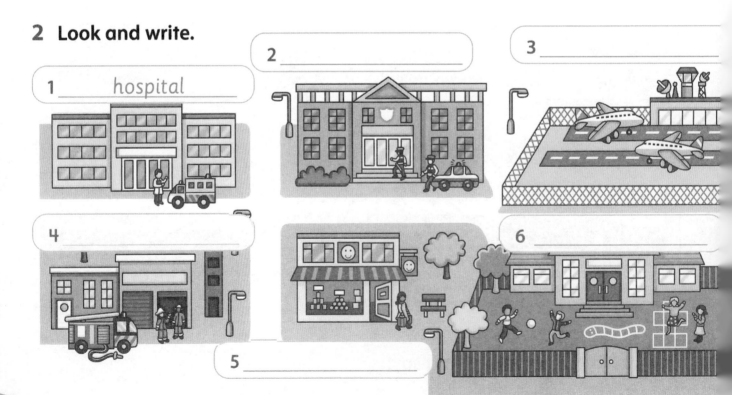

1 _____hospital_____

2 _____

3 _____

4 _____

5 _____

6 _____

1 Follow the maze and write.

| hospital | school | airport | ~~police station~~ | fire station | store |

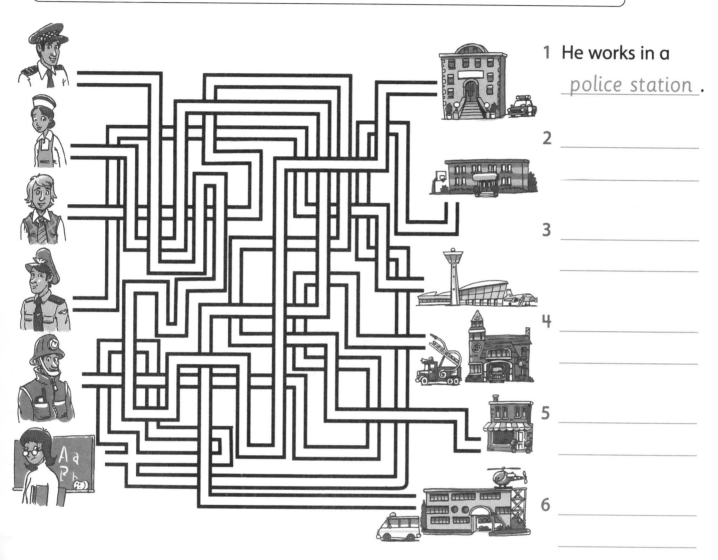

1 He works in a
   police station .

2 _____
   _____

3 _____
   _____

4 _____
   _____

5 _____
   _____

6 _____
   _____

Match.

(1) Does he work in a police station? [b]

(2) Does she work in a fire station? [ ]

(3) Does he work in a school? [ ]

(4) Does she work in a school? [ ]

a No, he doesn't.

b Yes, he does.

c No, she doesn't.

d Yes, she does.

1 Find and circle the words. supermarket   bank   ~~zoo~~   station

zoosupermarketstationbank

2 Look and write.

school   police station   fire station   station   ~~store~~
hospital   supermarket   garage   airport   zoo

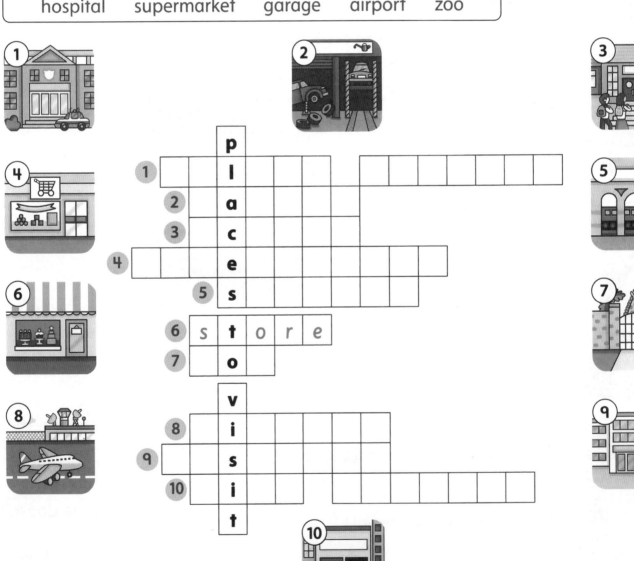

1 Order the letters.

① e c f a

face

② k l e a

③ l e a n p

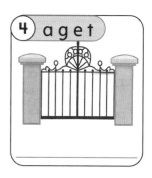
④ a g e t

2 Write.

lake   ~~gate~~   cake   face

Open the ¹ _____gate_____ .

See the ² _____ .

A smile on your ³ _____ .

Here is a ⁴ _____ .

3 Read. Circle the words with a_e. Underline the words with a.

①
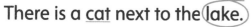

There is a <u>cat</u> next to the (lake.)

②

Open the gate. Here comes a van.

4 Now write the words in the correct box.

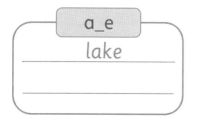
a_e

lake
_____

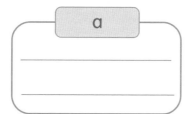
a

_____
_____

Skills Time!

Reading

1 Read.

I'm Jason. My dad works in an office. Every day he gets up at six o'clock. He puts on a white shirt, black pants, and a tie. He has breakfast. Then he goes to work by car.

In his office, my dad has a big table. His computer is on the table. He also has a photo of my mom, my sister, and me on his table. There is a box with pens and pencils.

He goes home at five o'clock and we all have dinner together at seven o'clock.

2 Read again. Circle three clothes words. Underline three family words.

3 Circle the incorrect word. Then write the sentence correctly.

1 Jason's dad works in a school.   *Jason's dad works in an office.*

2 He gets up at nine o'clock. _____

3 He puts on green pants. _____

4 He goes to work by train. _____

5 There are pens and apples in the box. _____

6 He goes home at three o'clock. _____

7 They have lunch at seven o'clock. _____

Writing

1 Write the sentences with commas (,) and *and*.

1 I like apples grapes bananas.

   I like apples, grapes, and bananas.

2 There are birds monkeys lions tigers.

   _____

3 We have English math science music.

   _____

4 He likes chicken pizza salad.

   _____

5 I get up have breakfast go to school.

   _____

 **About me!**

2 Circle the places where your family work.

| hospital | school | airport | police station | fire station |

| store | zoo | station | supermarket | bank | office | garage |

3 Draw and write about where your family works.

My mom works in a bank.

My _____ works in a _____.

My _____.

_____

_____

1 Write.

> No   doesn't   she   Yes   does   work   ~~Does~~   nurse

1 Does your mom work?

_____, she does.

2 Does she _____ in a bank?

No, she _____.

3 Does _____ work in a hospital?

Yes, she _____.

4 Is she a _____ ?

_____, she isn't. She's a doctor.

2 Read the words. Write them in the correct boxes.

> morning   ~~school~~   balloons   night   nuts   afternoon   garage
> evening   supermarket   candy   pastries   fire station

places	times	presents
school		

3 Circle the word that contains a different sound.
Write the word that is different.

1
    _cat_

2
      _____

3
      _____

4
       _____

4 Write.

| Yes, he does.   No, he doesn't. |

My name's Ted.
My dad is a pilot.
He works at night.

1  Does Ted's dad get up at eight o'clock?

No, he doesn't.

2  Does he go to bed at six o'clock?

_____

3  Does he have dinner at nine o'clock?

_____

4  Does he go home at one o'clock?

_____

10 It's hot today!

1 Match.

1 It's raining. [c]

2 It's windy. [ ]

3 It's hot. [ ]

4 It's cold. [ ]

5 It's snowing. [ ]

6 It's sunny. [ ]

a

b

c

d

e

f

2 Now write.

1

2

3

It's windy.   It's _____. _____

4

5

6

_____ _____ _____

1 Order the words.

1 | weather | What's | like | the | ? |

What's the weather like?

2 | your | . | on | Put | hats | sun |

_____

3 | put | Don't | . | your | on | coat |

_____

4 | umbrellas | have | don't | . | We | our |

_____

5 | window | close | Don't | the | . |

_____

6 | . | the | Open | door |

_____

2 Write [Put on   Don't put on]

①

It's cold. ____Put on____
your coat.

②

It's windy. _____
your hat.

③

It's raining. _____
your raincoat.

④

It's sunny. _____
your sunscreen.

⑤

It's snowing. _____
your shorts.

⑥

It's hot. _____
your coat.

1 Find and circle the weather words. Then write.

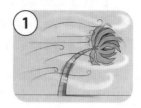

windy

s	n	o	w	i	n	g	★
u	r	a	i	n	i	n	g
n	h	w	i	n	d	y	★
n	o	★	c	o	l	d	★
y	t	★	★	★	★	★	★

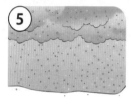

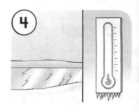

2 Now look and write.

play outside   ~~windy~~   snowing   go ice skating
sunny   fly a kite   make a snowman

1 When it's _____windy_____, we _____.

2 When it's _____, we _____ and we _____

3 When it's _____, we _____.

1 Order the letters.

1 k b i e
bike

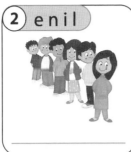
2 e n i l
_____

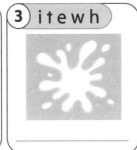
3 i t e w h
_____

4 e i k t
_____

5 n n e i
_____

2 Write.

| line   nine   ~~bike~~   kite   white |

Ride your ¹ ___bike___ . Fly your ² _____ .

The bike is red. The kite is ³ _____ .

White kite, white kite.

Count the children in the ⁴ _____ .

All together there are ⁵ _____ .

Nine in the line. Nine in the line.

3 Read. Circle the words with *i_e*. Underline the words with *i*.

1

Here are (nine) figs in a line.

2

There's a pig on my kite.

4 Now write the words in the correct box.

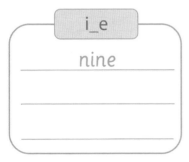
i_e
nine
_____
_____

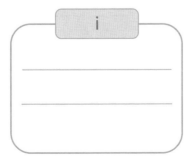
i
_____
_____
_____

Skills Time!

Reading

1 Read.

> It's playtime. It's very hot and sunny outside. Wear your sun hats, please. Don't put on your coats.

> It's P.E. time in the sports field. Don't put on your tracksuits. It's too hot. Put on your P.E. shorts and T-shirts.

> It's home time. It's raining and windy now. Put on your raincoats and take your umbrellas. Don't wear your hats. They can blow away. See you tomorrow.

2 Read again. Write the weather.

1 It's playtime. What's the weather like? _____

2 It's P.E. time. What's the weather like? _____

3 It's home time. What's the weather like? _____

3 Read again and check (✔).

	playtime	P.E. time	home time
1 Don't put on your coats.	✔		
2 Don't wear your hats.			
3 Put on your raincoats.			
4 Wear your sun hats.			
5 Don't put on your tracksuits.			
6 Put on your shorts and T-shirts.			
7 Take your umbrellas.			

Writing

1 Write the words in the correct boxes.

wear   cold   tired
go   ride   hungry
thirsty   eat
sunny   drink

verbs

wear

_____

_____

_____

_____

adjectives

_____

_____

_____

_____

About me!

2 Circle today's weather. What can you do? Write ✔ or ✘.

raining   windy   hot   cold   snowing   sunny

go outside ☐   fly a kite ☐   make a snowman ☐   go ice skating ☐

wear a coat ☐   wear a sun hat ☐   take an umbrella ☐

3 Draw and write about the weather and the things you can and can't do.

Today it's sunny. I can go outside.

Today, it's _____.

I can _____.

_____

I can't _____.

_____

85

Fluency Time! ④

1 Look and write. ask ~~Are~~ free about fine after listen

1
_____Are_____ you free _____ school today?

Sorry, I'm not _____ today.

2
How _____ on Thursday?

Yes, that's _____.

3
I'll _____ my dad.

4
We can _____ to music.

Great. I love music.

2 Order the words.

1 free | Are | you | school | ? | after

Are you free after school?

2 not | . | I'm | free | , | Sorry

_____

3 on | How | ? | Wednesday | about

_____

4 ask | mom | I'll | my | .

1 Watch and match. ▶

1

2

3

a It's eleven o'clock.

b Sorry. I'm not free today.

c Are you free after school today?

2 Watch again. Complete.

about	can	ask	free	Oops	not

1

Are you __free__ after school today?

Sorry. I'm _____ free today.

2

How _____ on Tuesday?

3

We _____ play with my dollhouse.

Great! I'll _____ my mom.

4

_____!

3 Talk with a friend. What do you play at home?

I play soccer with my brother.

Lesson One Words

1 Number the picture.

1. ~~skirt~~
2. scarf
3. gloves
4. jeans
5. boots
6. shirt

2 Now look and write.

This is   These are

①

These are gloves.

②

This is a _____

③

④

⑤

⑥

1 **Write.**

skirt   scarf   gloves   ~~jeans~~   boots   shirt

He's wearing jeans.

She's _____ .

_____

_____

_____

_____

2 **Write.**   dress   is   ~~What~~   I'm   T-shirt   wearing   He's

What are you wearing?

_____ wearing a _____ .

And Jim?
What _____
he _____ ?

_____ wearing a _____ .

1 Read and draw the times on the clocks.

It's three o'clock.

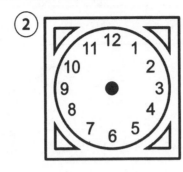

It's two thirty.

It's eight fifteen.

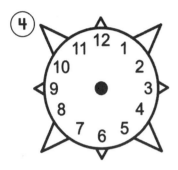

It's nine forty-five.

It's eleven o'clock.

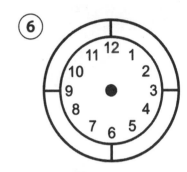

It's nine thirty.

2 Look at the clocks and write the times.

It's four fifteen.

It's _____

_____

_____

_____

_____

_____

_____

_____

1 Order the letters.

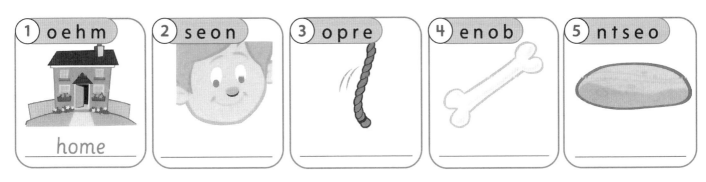

1 o e h m — home
2 s e o n —
3 o p r e —
4 e n o b —
5 n t s e o —

2 Write.

| nose ~~rope~~ stone bone home |

The fox has my ¹ _rope_ .

The fox is on a ² _____ .

Hurry up, fox.

I want to go ³ _____ .

My ⁴ _____ is cold.

Here is a ⁵ _____ .

Hurry up, fox.

3 Read. Circle the words with o_e. Underline the words with o.

1

A fox has a (bone.)

2

There is a mop in my home.

4 Now write the words in the correct box.

o_e	o
bone	

Skills Time!

Reading

1 Read.

Where is my friend?

I'm at the station.
Where is my friend?
At the front of the train?
Or is she at the end?

Where is Lucy?
Is she wearing a skirt?
Is she wearing her jeans?
Or wearing a shirt?

Here is my friend.
She has a toy cow.
I say, "Hello, Lucy,"
And we're both happy now.

2 Read again. Circle three clothes words. Underline one toy.

3 Read again and circle the correct word. Write.

1 The girl is at the ___station___ .

| farm | station | zoo | school |

2 She can't see her _____ .

| aunt | mom | friend | sister |

3 Her friend's name is _____ .

| Katie | Sally | Milly | Lucy |

4 Lucy is on the _____ .

| swings | bus | train | slide |

5 Her friend has a toy _____ .

| goat | car | rabbit | cow |

6 Lucy and her friend are _____ .

| sad | happy | angry | scared |

Writing

1 Look and write. | fifteen   forty-five |

1 It's six ___forty-five___ .

2 It's three _____ .

3 It's nine _____ .

4 It's ten _____ .

5 It's three _____ .

6 It's two _____ .

 About me!

2 Look and circle the clothes you are wearing now. Write the colors.

skirt _____	pants _____	shirt _____	T-shirt _____
shoes _____	boots _____	jeans _____	socks _____
scarf _____	shorts _____	dress _____	hat _____

Draw and write about the clothes you are wearing.

___I'm wearing a blue shirt.___

I'm wearing _____ .

I'm _____ .

_____

_____

_____

Social Studies Time!

1 Unscramble the words.

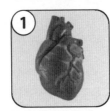 ① e a t r h _____

 ② b e t h a r _____

 ③ d e n b _____

 ④ s l s m u c e _____

 ⑤ y x g o n e _____

2 Write.

breathe   ~~fun~~   oxygen   muscles   exercises   bend

1 Exercise is _____*fun*_____ and good for you.

2 When you _____, you get oxygen from the air.

3 A strong heart means more _____ around the body.

4 Strong _____ mean you can lift heavy things.

5 A flexible body means you can _____ more easily.

6 Running, playing soccer, and swimming are great _____.

1 Listen again. Write. 🎧 132

Exercise   run   park   play   sister   horses   skate   muscles

_____Exercise_____ is good for you.

Yes, I know. It's good for your heart and your _____.

What exercise do you do?

I _____ and play in the _____ every day after school. What about you, Ben?

I _____ soccer and I _____. I have really cool skates.

What about your big _____?

She rides _____.

2 Look at Exercise 1. Point and say.

12 You're sleeping!

1 Find and circle the words.

invitation   cake   ~~wedding~~   guests   band   bride

w e d d i n g c a k e b r i d e b a n d i n v i t a t i o n g u e s t s

2 Look and write.

invitation   wedding   ~~cake~~   eat   sing   guests
dance   bride   band   dress

① c a k e

② _ _ _ t _ _ _ _ _

③ _ _ t

h

④ _ _ e _ _ _

w

⑤ _ e _ _ _

⑥ d _ _

⑦ d _ _ _

⑧ _ _ i _

⑨ _ _ n _

⑩ _ _ g _

1 **Look at the picture. Order the questions and write the answers.**

No, they aren't.   ~~Yes, they are.~~   No, she isn't.   Yes, she is.   No, he isn't.

 1 they dancing Are ?

Are they dancing?

Yes, they are.

 2 singing ? she Is

 3 he Is ? eating

 4 she ? sleeping Is

5 drinking Are they ?

2 **Now point and say.**

They're dancing.
She's …

1 Match.

1 make   b   a a dress

2 wash   ☐   b a cake

3 choose   ☐   c photos

4 take   ☐   d the car

2 Circle the correct word and write.

1 Mom is ___making___ cakes.   (making) washing wearing

2 Dad is _____ the car.   brushing washing choosing

3 My cousin is _____ lots of photos.   taking making washing

4 My sister is _____ a dress.   washing choosing brushing

5 I'm _____ my hair.   taking washing brushing

1 Order the letters.

① u n J e

June

② b u e c

_____

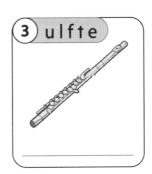
③ u l f t e

_____

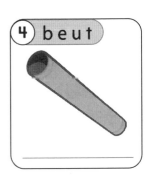
④ b e u t

_____

2 Write.

| tube   June   flute   cube |

This month is ¹ _____June_____

And it's my birthday!

I have a fun ² _____ ,

I can play all day.

I have a new ³ _____

For my birthday,

And a poster in a ⁴ _____ .

What a happy day!

3 Read. Circle the words with u_e. Underline the words with u.

①

This (mule) can run.

②

I have a flute and I'm sitting on a rug.

4 Now write the words in the correct box.

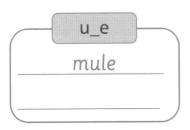
u_e

mule

_____

_____

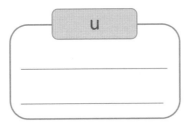
u

_____

_____

Reading

1 Read.

Dear Bella,

Thank you for your email. We are all fine. I really like your green and white dress. Enjoy the party!
Here is my big news. My aunt has a new baby! It's a boy and he is three weeks old. His name is James. He's very small and he has blue eyes. He doesn't have any hair yet.
Here is a picture of my aunt and uncle with baby James. He's wearing a small hat and little white boots. All of my family is very, very happy.

Love from
Hannah

2 Circle the incorrect word. Then write the sentence correctly.

1 Hannah likes Bella's (jeans.)   *Hannah likes Bella's dress.*

2 Hannah's aunt has a new car.   _____

3 The baby is very big.   _____

4 The baby is a girl.   _____

5 His name is Max.   _____

6 He has brown eyes.   _____

7 He's wearing a scarf.   _____

8 His boots are red.   _____

Writing

1 Complete the sentences with *ing*.

1   **wear**
He's ___wearing___
white boots.

2   **watch**
We're _____
TV.

3   **do**
My sister is _____
her homework.

4   **eat**
She's _____
her dinner.

5   **listen**
We're _____ to
music.

6   **look**
We're _____
at cakes.

About me!

2 Circle the things you can see people doing at a party.

> eating   riding a bike   drinking   dancing   swimming
>
> listening to music   playing soccer   talking   singing

3 Draw and write about your family at a party.

I'm at a party. I'm _____.

I'm _____.

I'm _____.

My mom is _____.

My dad is _____.

_____

1 **Look and write.**

I'm wearing   boots   a scarf   jeans   a shirt   a hat   gloves

1 I'm wearing jeans
and _____ .

2 I'm wearing _____
and _____ .

3 I'm wearing _____
_____
_____ .

2 **Read the words. Write them in the correct boxes.**

cake   jeans   windy   invitation   skirt   raining
present   sunny   boots   hot   bride   scarf

weather	wedding	clothes
windy		

3 Say the words. Check (✔) two words that rhyme.

4 Look and write.

1 drinking
2 eating
3 talking
4 singing
5 dancing
6 playing

1 _He's drinking._

2 _____

3 _____

4 _____

5 _____

6 _____

13 Look at all the animals!

1 Look and number.

(1)	~~cow~~
(2)	goat
(3)	horse
(4)	sheep
(5)	donkey
(6)	goose

2 Now write.

(1) There's a ___cow___ behind the gate.

(2) There's a _____ next to the gate.

(3) There's a _____ in front of the house.

(4) There's a _____ between the horse and the van.

(5) There's a _____ behind the tree.

(6) There's a _____ on the van.

1 Write.

shorter than   ~~bigger than~~   taller than   smaller than

1 big   _bigger than_

2 small   _____

3 short   _____

4 tall   _____

2 Write the opposites. Then write the sentences.

bigger _____   taller _____

A horse is ___bigger than___ a goose.
A goose is _____ a horse.

Rosy _____.
Billy _____.

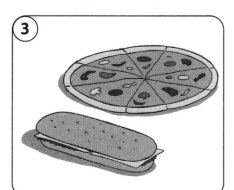

A pizza is _____.
_____.

1 Find and circle the words.

slow   ~~fast~~   quiet   loud

(fast)loudquietslow

2 Look and write.

~~louder~~   quieter   slower   faster

HONK!

Cluck

1 goose _louder_   2 sheep _____   3 cow _____   4 hen _____

3 Look and write.

1 The goose is ___louder than___ the hen.

2 The sheep is _____ the cow.

3 The cow is _____ the sheep.

4 The hen is _____ the goose.

1 **Order the letters.**

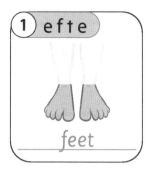

① e f t e

feet

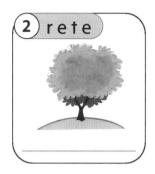

② r e t e

_____

③ e e h t r

_____

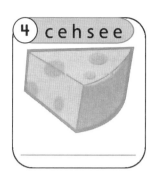

④ c e h s e e

_____

2 **Write.** feet   cheese   ~~tree~~   three

Look up at the green ¹_____tree_____.

What can you see?

Two ²_____ and a tail.

Count them, one, two, ³_____!

A monkey with a piece of ⁴_____,

That's what's hiding there!

3 **Read. Circle the words with *ee*. Underline the words with *e*.**

①

This pen is green.

②

There are three monkeys
in the tree.

③

My bed is red.

4 **Now write the words in the correct box.**

ee

green

_____

_____

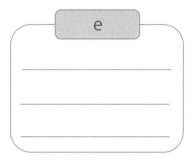

e

_____

_____

_____

Skills Time!

Reading

1 Read.

Katie and Harry live at Fig Farm. On the farm they grow vegetables: carrots, tomatoes, and potatoes. They have fruit trees too: apples, plums, and figs. There are also animals on the farm: hens, cows, goats, and sheep. They get eggs and meat from the hens. They get milk and meat from the cows. They get milk and meat from the goats. And they get wool and meat from the sheep.

There are also two dogs and four cats on the farm. Katie and Harry help their family on the farm.

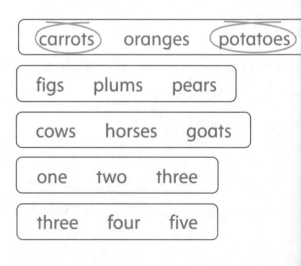

2 Read and circle.

1 Circle two vegetables on the farm.   carrots   oranges   potatoes

2 Circle two fruit trees on the farm.   figs   plums   pears

3 Circle two animals on the farm.   cows   horses   goats

4 How many dogs are there on the farm?   one   two   three

5 How many cats are there on the farm?   three   four   five

Writing

1 Circle _and_. Then write two sentences for each sentence.

1 Harry is seven (and) Katie is nine.   _Harry is seven. Katie is nine._

2 This is a donkey and these are hens.   _____

3 I like bananas and he likes apples.   _____

4 There is a slide and there are swings. _____

About me!

2 Circle the animals you can see at a farm.

lion   cow   sheep   tiger   giraffe   donkey   horse   zebra

hen   chick   monkey   elephant   goat   goose   polar bear

3 Draw and write about a farm visit.

At a farm, I can see a goat.

At a farm, I can see a _____.

I can see a _____.

I _____.

_____.

_____.

I can't see a _____.

I can't see a _____.

I _____.

Fluency Time! ⑤

1 Look and write.

| for | Everyone's | welcome | in | room | ~~party~~ | having | Thank |

1 Welcome to the ___party___ .
Come _____ .
_____ in the dining _____ .

2 This is _____ you.
_____ you.

Thank you for _____ me.

3 You're _____ .

2 Write the sentences. Use the word(s) in the box.

1 Welcome to the party.

   my house _Welcome to my house._

2 This is for you.

   Grandpa _____ .

3 Everyone's in the living room.

   kitchen _____ .

4 Grandpa is in the kitchen.

   Your aunt _____ .

1 Watch and check (✔) the objects you see.

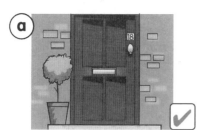

(a) ✔

(b)  ☐

(c)  ☐

(d)  ☐

(e)  ☐

(f) 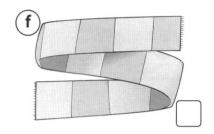 ☐

2 Watch again. Write the sentences and match.

(a)

1 party / the / Welcome / to
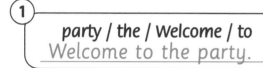
Welcome to the party.

2 for / this / you / is / Ellie,
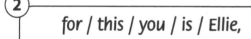
_____ .

(b)

3 you / having / Thank / me / for
_____ .

(c)

4 soon, / See / Ellie / you
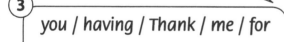
_____ .

(d)

3 Choose and color a present for your family.
Tell your friend.

> This is for my sister.
> She likes dolls.

Lesson One Words

1 Find and circle the words.

| photo | dry | ~~kind~~ | wet | fridge | bad |

 **1** k s e (k i n d) p y

 **2** o c t w e t x y

 **3** t p d r y q x

 **4** h s p h o t o x b

 **5** l e p b a d v c

 **6** p u f r i d g e t e

2 Now look and write.

1 There are some _____photos_____ on the _____.

2 This boy is _____.

3 This duck is very _____.

4 Her hands are _____.

5 His hands are _____.

1 Order the words.

1 bad were The ducks . _The ducks were bad._

2 was good . This boy _____

3 park were We the in . _____

4 babies . The weren't sad _____

5 were hungry They . _____

6 . dry was Mom _____

7 wet wasn't She . _____

8 then little Billy was . _____

2 Look and write.

| was | wasn't | were | weren't |

1 Rosy and Tim ___were___ in the park.

2 Tim _____ very kind. The babies _____ cold. They _____ hungry.

3 It was raining. Rosy and Tim _____ very wet. Mom _____ wet. She _____ dry.

4 The ducks _____ very bad. The goat _____ bad too.

5 Billy _____ a bad boy. But he's a good boy now.

1 Find and circle the words.

neat   trash   ~~floor~~   messy

f l o o r m e s s y t r a s h n e a t

2 Look and write.

happy   photo   wet   ~~hungry~~   party   dry
dirty   floor   neat

①

③

⑤

⑦

⑨

1	h	u	n	g	r	y
2		a				
3		p				
4		p				
5						y

m
6 e
m
7 o
8 r
i
9 e
s

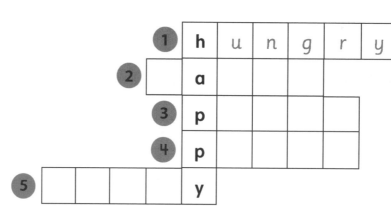

②

④

⑥

⑧

1 Read the words. Add the magic e and write.

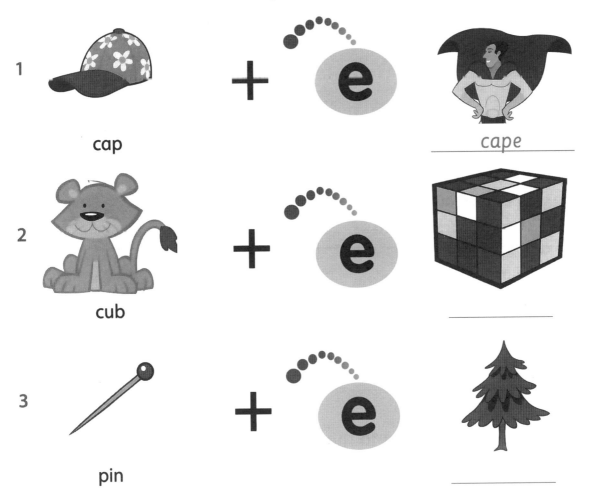

1 cap   + e   cape

2 cub   + e   _____

3 pin   + e   _____

2 Write. | ~~cube~~   Cub   cap   pine   cape   pin   Cube |

A lion cub plays with a ¹ _cube._

² _____, cub, cub,

³ _____, cube, cube.

There's a big ⁴ _____ under the ⁵ _____.

Pin, pin, pin.

Pine, pine, pine.

She has a red ⁶ _____ and a ⁷ _____.

Cap, cap, cap.

Cape, cape, cape.

Skills Time!

Reading

1 Read.

Our class play by Robin (Class 2L)
This year, our class play was On the farm.
My friends and I were the farm animals.
I was a horse. My costume was a big
horse s head and body. Charles was a
sheep. Nicola was a hen. All the animals
were happy on the farm.

Everyone was very good. All our moms and
dads were very happy. Our teacher was
very proud of us.

2 Read again. Match the children to the animals.

1 Robin   b   a hen

2 Nicola   [ ]   b horse

3 Charles [ ]   c sheep

3 Now complete the sentences.

| sheep | good | 2L | animals | hen | happy |

1 Robin is in class _____2L_____.

2 Robin and his friends were farm _____.

3 Charles was a _____.

4 Nicola was a _____.

5 Everyone was very _____.

6 The moms and dads were _____.

Writing

1 Write *and* or *or*.

1 I have a teddy bear ___and___ a doll.

2 He doesn't have a kite _____ a bike.

3 I am cold _____ tired.

4 She isn't scared _____ angry.

5 He doesn't like candy _____ chocolate.

6 She doesn't play soccer _____ tennis.

7 I do my homework _____ watch TV.

8 I like apples _____ pears.

 **About me!**

2 Circle how you were during 2nd grade. Underline how your friends were.

happy	sad	kind	bad	neat	messy
good	tired	angry	scared	brave	

3 Draw and write about you and your friends during 2nd grade.

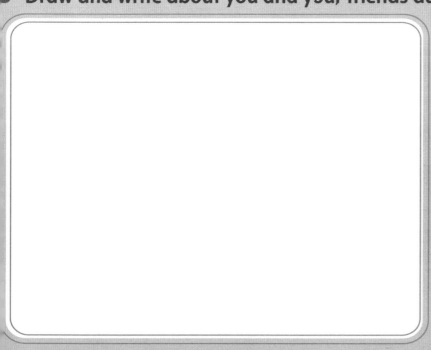

I was happy.

I was _____.

I _____.

_____

_____

My friends were _____.

They were _____.

They _____.

_____

Geography Time!

1   Match the words to the meanings.

1 camel

2 sand dune

3 leaf

4 plant

5 rock

a They take water from under the ground.

b It can live for a week without water.

c It is a very big stone.

d The wind blows this mountain shape.

e This is part of a plant.

2   Write.

> plant   ~~sand~~   snow   camel   leaves   rocks   rain

There are three types of desert. Some have  _____sand_____ . Some

have 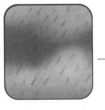 _____ . Some have ice and _____ .

There is very little  _____ in the desert. Animals like the

 _____ don't drink every day. A cactus is a desert

_____ . It has lots of water in its  _____ .

1 Listen again and write the sentences. 🎵 170

1 This | and | desert | is | . | hot | sandy | a

   This is a hot and sandy desert.

2 can | on | sand | walk | the | Camels | .

   _____

3 is | . | ice | snow | and | There | everywhere

   _____

4 are | cold | desert | bears | and | There | foxes | in | . | the

   _____

5 rocks | This | has | lots | of | . | desert | big

   _____

6 deserts | There | . | sand | dunes | in | windy | usually | are

   _____

2 Match the pictures to the sentences in Exercise 1.

 3 □
 □ □
 □
 □

3 Look at Exercise 1. Point and say.

15 Good job!

1 Write.

| man | men | woman | women | ~~child~~ | children |

① child

②

③

④

⑤

⑥

2 Now look and answer the questions.

| There is | There are |

1 How many men are there?

There are two men.

2 How many children are there?

3 How many boys are there?

4 How many women are there?

Write. | some any |

①

There were _some_ chairs in the classroom.

②

There weren't _____ tables in the school yard.

③

There weren't _____ children in the art room.

④

There were _____ teachers on the field.

Look and write.

| some ~~were~~ school yard was any wasn't |

①

It was the school awards ceremony.

They _____ _were_ _____ late.

②

They were in the classroom. There weren't _____ children.

But there were _____ teachers.

③

The awards ceremony _____ in the classroom. It was in the _____.

④

There _____ an award for English. Rosy and Tim were the winners.

1 Match.

1 first   c   a 3rd

2 second   b 4th

3 third   c 1st

4 fourth   d 2nd

2 Find and circle.

fourth   ~~first~~   third   second   finish line

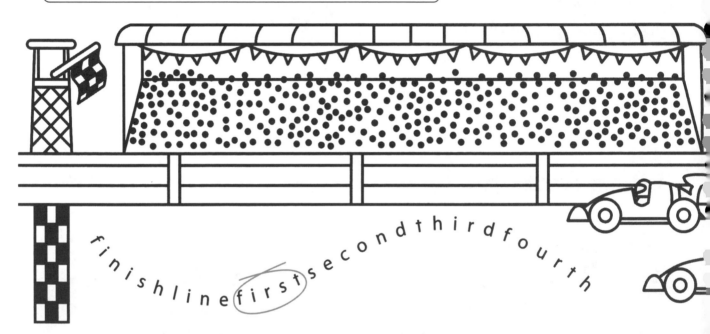

finishline (first) second third fourth

3 Look and write. Use the words above.

The animals were in a race!

Go, go, go!

Some were fast,

And some were slow.

The hen was _____.

The rabbit was _____.

The cow was _____.

The horse was _____.

1 Circle the word that contains a different end sound.

1 bank   drink   (swing)   2 ring   bank   pink

3 swing   king   drink   4 king   pink   swing

5 drink   ring   king

2 Match the letters and write.

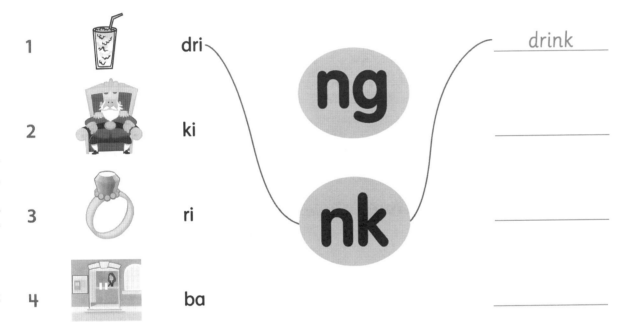

1   dri   **ng**   _drink_

2   ki   _____

3   ri   **nk**   _____

4   ba   _____

3 Write. | Swing   Ring   Drink   ~~Sing~~   king |

1 _Sing_ a song while you
2 _____, swing, swing.
Look at the 3 _____ with his
4 _____, ring, ring.
Now you're thirsty, have a
5 _____, drink, drink.

Skills Time!

Reading

1 Read the story about Suzy the horse again. Put the pictures in the correct order.

2 Match the sentences to the pictures above.

1 Suzy is a carousel horse. `b`

2 She isn't happy. She wants to be a real horse.

3 She can move her head and tail. She is a real horse.

4 Suzy is happy. She's running and eating.

5 Now she is cold and scared.

6 Suzy goes back to the carousel.

3 Circle the incorrect words. Write the sentence correctly.

1 Suzy is a (cow.)

   Suzy is a horse.

2 She's behind a green horse.

3 She's in front of a blue goat.

4 She drinks milk in the field.

5 She eats ice cream in the field.

6 At night she's hot.

Writing

1 Write s or les.

1 family ___families___   2 boy _____

3 baby _____   4 turkey _____

5 party _____   6 monkey _____

 **About me!**

2 Check (✔) what you can see at a school open day.

men ☐   rabbits ☐   women ☐   children ☐

lions ☐   teachers ☐   frogs ☐

3 Draw and write about a school open day.

There are some children.

There are some _____

_____.

There _____

_____.

There _____

_____.

There aren't any _____

_____.

There _____

_____.

There _____

_____.

1 Write.

I'm the winner!

1 short   The boy is ___shorter than___ the girl.

2 small   His coat is _____ the girl's coat.

3 fast   But he is _____ the girl.

4 loud   And he is _____ the girl.

5 quiet   The girl is _____ the boy.

2 Read the words. Write them in the correct boxes.

cow	fourth	goat	first	horse	~~bad~~	sheep
dry	third	dirty	wet	second		

adjectives

bad
_____
_____
_____

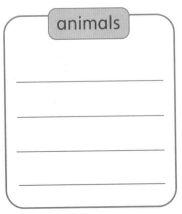

animals

_____
_____
_____
_____

numbers

_____
_____
_____
_____

3 **Look and write how many.**

women	2
dolls	___
men	___
children	___
teddy bears	___
toy cars	___

4 **Now look and write.**

> There are some ...   There aren't any ...

1 women   *There are some women.*

2 dolls   _____

3 men   _____

4 children   _____

5 teddy bears _____

6 toy cars   _____

5 **Answer the questions.**

1 What's your name? _____

2 How many brothers and sisters do you have? _____

3 What are you wearing? _____

4 What color are your clothes? _____

5 What is your teacher wearing? _____

6 What color are his or her clothes? _____

7 What are you doing now? _____

Picture dictionary

Look and write.

Starter Welcome back!

___ ___ ___ ___

___ ___ ___ ___

1 School things

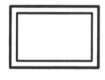    

___ ___ ___ ___ ___ ___

___ ___ ___ ___ ___

2 Feelings

3 Outdoor activities

4 Food

5 School subjects

2 + 2 = 4	3 x 2 = 6
6 − 3 = 3	4 + 5 = 9
7 x 1 = 7	5 + 3 = 8

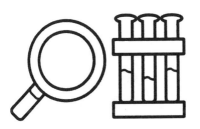

6 After-school activities

_____ _____ _____ _____ _____

_____ _____ _____ _____

7 Special days

   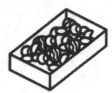

_____ _____ _____ _____ _____

 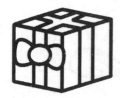  

_____ _____ _____ _____

8 Everyday activities

9 Places

10 Weather

11 Clothes

12 Celebrations

13 Farm animals

14 Memories

15 People